Lose the Booze

the no-meetings guide to clearing up your drinking
problem, for good

by
Margaret Gold

CHAPTER ONE:

ABOUT THIS BOOK

SO....YOU THINK maybe you're drinking too much.

This book is for you if you'd like to quit, but don't think that any number of steps will get you there.

We used the science available today, not the ideas of the 1930s that are promoted by 12-step groups, to create a guide for the drinker who wants to stop using too much alcohol.

Relying on scientific data from more than 40 peer-reviewed, tested studies, we'll offer you a map out of your darkness and into sunlight.

Maybe you are a veteran of failed attempts to cut back on your drinking. Maybe someone you love has told you that you drink too much, or that drinking makes you a different person. Maybe you've been told by a court that some misbehavior you committed while you were drinking is a sign that you have a drinking problem—and that may be true, and you should certainly assess your alcohol use and follow the signs toward moderation.

If you want to stop having problems with alcohol, the tools and ideas in this book can help.

To stop drinking, you'll need to do a few things.

1) Understand your patterns of alcohol use

2) Figure out what alcohol is doing for you

3) Make your plan to replace alcohol's benefits with other solutions, that don't hurt more than they help.

Before you toss aside this book, use the test in Chapter 2 to evaluate your drinking.

Learn how you got the idea that the 'lifelong abstinence' is the only right treatment for problem drinking...and other important facts about addiction...in Chapter 3.

Before you start learning about addiction, the history of alcohol treatment, how alcohol trains and changes your brain and behaviors, and how to quit: The simple solution may be to drink less. If you choose to cut back or quit, what challenges will you face? Maybe your drinking is safe for you. One way to find out is to stop using alcohol for a week or two.

If that sounds impossible to you, because you've tried to cut back before— read about structured reduction in Chapter 4 and give it a try.

Chapter 5 reviews the science on how alcohol works in your brain, slowing things down and etching on its results, giving you a drinking habit.

In Chapter 6, you'll learn how alcohol affects your brain and body. Did you learn this stuff in health class in high school? Maybe, but depending on how long it's been since high school, the science may have come a long way.

Chapter 7 describes the common psychology of problem drinkers, and some tips and tricks to identify and manage your feelings without liquor.

Diet, exercise and sleep are critical parts of any intentional strategy to end alcohol problems. Of course, there will be days when you don't feel delighted about changing your drinking habit, and for those times, you'll want your motivation to be held out in front of you like the carrot.

After you've learned all this, you'll make your 7 day plan, customized for your drinking habit.

It's not easy to change a habit, and you may have trouble at first. But there are many ways to work on your drinking problem—the important thing is, you've chosen one and you're getting started.

If you have been referred to a 12-step program by a court, because you broke the law while drunk, this book's companion volume will be available soon. You can't be sentenced to attending religious services, and 12-step programs ask their members to pray, turn their problem over to a higher power, and other spiritual remedies for their drinking problems. In addition to the lack of scientific support for 'working the steps' as a method to end problem drinking, in the US, we don't send people to church as a punishment for their bad behaviors. Look for The Northstar Guide to Court-Ordered 12 Step, coming soon.

CHAPTER TWO:

TAKE THE TEST: IS THIS BOOK FOR YOU?

THIS QUIZ IS based on a screening test, written by the National Institutes of Health, and handed out by doctors and therapists to their patients. So you can tell a lot about whether you need to look at your drinking in private, at home, right now. No need to wait for a clinic visit. Of course, be honest with yourself —you can't choose a strategy for managing your drinking problem until you know more.

Part 1: How much or often are you using alcohol?
How often do you have a drink?
- ○ Never
- ○ Monthly or less
- ○ 2 to 4 times a month
- ○ 2 to 3 times a week
- ● 4 or more times a week

How many drinks do you have on a typical day when you are drinking?
- ○ 1 or 2
- ○ 3 or 4
- ● 5 or 6
- ○ 7 to 9
- ○ 10 or more

How often do you have 5 or more drinks on one occasion?
- ○ Never
- ○ Less than monthly
- ○ Weekly
- ● Daily or almost daily

If you can truly answer 'Never' to the first question, you should put down this e-book and go outside to enjoy some sunshine. Play online solitaire. Walk your dog. Or whatever. This book is not for you. (If you bought it for someone else, please note that you can take the quiz for your loved one, but you can't get sober for anyone else.) But if you're drinking more often than you want to be, or ever have more than 5 drinks at a time, it's worth continuing.

Some people can drink quantities of booze that would stun an elephant on certain occasions, yet never drink more than they planned or feel badly about their alcohol use. As long as their lives aren't being impacted by their drinking, they're fine. So how do you know if you have a problem? Let's explore problem habits in Part 2.

Part 2: How you see your alcohol use
How often during the last year have you found that you were not able to stop drinking once you had started? For example, you planned to have a drink or two but spent the evening or weekend impaired by alcohol?
- ○ Never
- ○ Less than monthly
- ● Weekly
- ○ Daily or almost daily

How often during the last year have you had a feeling of remorse after drinking? Do you find that you're kicking yourself for once again having had more liquor than you can handle?
- ○ Never
- ○ Monthly
- ● Weekly

Do you plan social, family or work events around alcohol? Are you ever preoccupied by thinking about where and when you can have your next drink?

These questions help you to explore how you feel about your alcohol use. If you're a heavy user of alcohol (part 1) but still manage to function well, you might want to cut back. On the other hand, even if you're "only" a light user (never more than 5 drinks, less than monthly) you may still have a drinking problem. If you feel badly about your drinking, worry about it, or can't control your drinking once you start, move ahead to Part 3.

Part 3: How's that working for you? Objective measures of a drinking problem.
How often do you fail to do what's expected of you after drinking? Have you

missed work, forgotten to pick up your kids, misplaced something (like your car, parked while you were sober)?

- ☞ Never
- ○ Less than monthly
- ○ Monthly
- ○ Weekly

How often do you need a first drink in the morning to get yourself going?

- ○ Monthly
- ○ Weekly NEVER
- ○ Daily or almost daily

Have you forgotten what happened during a drinking episode? If you've ever had a blackout, is it something that seems to happen to you…

- ○ Monthly
- ○ Weekly ONCE A YEAR
- ○ Daily or almost daily

Do you drink alone? Is *any* of your drinking a secret from family members, friends or loved ones?

Have you, or someone else, had problems connected to your drinking? Some common problems: DUI, fighting or other problems with the law, physical injury, loss of job, forgetting to pay bills… NO

Has a relative, friend, doctor, or co-worker expressed concern about your drinking recently, or suggested you cut down? yes

Some warning signs are subtle: working your way through the bottle of wine once it's been uncorked. Finishing the six-pack "to recycle all the bottles at once". Celebrating your sister's cousin-in-law's half birthday with a drink: on the bubble.

The questions in Part 3 focus on objective, black and white feedback from your body (blackouts and hair of the dog drinking are signs of alcohol abuse and physical dependence, respectively) and the wider world.

Quiz results

- ○ If you are blacking out, you have a drinking problem.
- ○ If you need a drink to get up more than once in a very blue moon, you

have a drinking problem.

- ○ If you are drinking in secret, you have a drinking problem and an integrity problem, because you're also withholding information from your friends & family to avoid conflicts about your drinking. (Otherwise it wouldn't be a secret, right?)
- ○ If you've been arrested, in a fight, fallen or knocked someone down, threatened with job loss if you call in hung over one more time, counseled about your drinking by your doctor, HR department at work… you've got a drinking problem.

So what's next? Moderating or stopping your drinking.

Warning: If you're dependent on alcohol, you can experience alcohol withdrawal symptoms if you suddenly stop drinking. These physical symptoms include:

- ○ hand tremors ('the shakes')
- ○ sweating
- ○ nausea
- ○ visual hallucinations (seeing things that are not actually real)
- ○ seizures (fits)

If you start to experience any of these, get yourself to a doctor. Right now. Seriously, put down your e-reader and get medical help if you have quit cold turkey and have these symptoms. You need medical detoxification, a planned and supervised transition from alcohol abuse to an alcohol-free body. Don't try to go it alone if you have withdrawal symptoms—you can be seriously injured by your body's best efforts to keep things stable without your regular dose of liquor.

CHAPTER THREE:

ADDICTION: A HISTORY

SOME SOBER PEOPLE (you may have met one or two) seem to think everyone who uses alcohol has a drinking problem. A problem that can solved by attending meetings, lots of meetings, in smoky rooms full of other people who have drinking problems. Meetings that offer terrible coffee, that ask you to tithe a dollar. Meetings at which criminals—people who broke the law while drunk are called criminals, not alcoholics—tell sad stories and ask someone to sign a note for the court that supervises their rehabilitation.

Before you take that walk down the steps into the church basement, though, it's probably a good idea to have a broader perspective. Do you have a drinking problem? If you think so, you deserve to know what the options are to get better.

There is a terrible, well-kept secret about 12-step programs that you may not know: They don't work.

Yes, for the people who regularly attend meetings, AND stop using alcohol completely, they appear to work just fine. This is not an example of treatment method that works, as much as it's an example of sampling bias. Unless you've heard from nine drop-outs for everyone who swears that 12-step saved their lives, though, the sample of testimony about whether meetings 'work' doesn't reflect anything but the opinions of people for whom it 'worked'.

Here's a hard number, from a textbook used in training addiction counselors: For 92% of alcohol abusers who try 12-step, it's just one more strategy that fails to support sobriety. It's true that alcoholics who choose to regularly attend

Alcoholics Anonymous meetings drink less than alcoholics who don't. However, that doesn't demonstrate that AA meetings "work", but instead that alcoholics who find AA helpful in managing their drinking tend to go back to AA.

Speculatively, perhaps AA can "work" for drinkers who rely on a bar for their social contacts. Replace the smoky place that serves alcohol with the smoky room in which alcohol isn't served, replace the drunks on barstools with former drunks who want to help the problem drinker quit, and you've provided a new social circle for the drinker. A place to go to spend time with like-minded people and not drink? That seems reasonable, for that type of alcohol abuser.

Studies show that social support and a sense of purpose in life, both provided at AA meetings, are important factors in lasting recovery from addiction; in that sense, 12-step attendance may provide some help to some addicts.

Guesses and intuition are the best we can do to analyze 12-step's uneven results, though. Attempts to produce valid scientific support for AA, as a strategy for treating alcoholism that's better than nothing, haven't been successful. Again, more than 9 of 10 people who decide to try AA when they want to quit drinking continue to attend. Of the remaining 8% who keep coming back, because, as they are told at the end of each meeting, "It works!", all are not successfully, permanently abstinent from alcohol. The phenomenon of that guy who doesn't drink for some length of days adding up to years, then 'slips', is well known among 12-steppers.

In fact, most addicts recover on their own. Of diagnosed alcoholics, seen by doctors, under the watch of researchers, only 25 percent were still considered alcoholics a year into the study—regardless of what approach to recovery they took. So 75% of drinkers, suffering from what AA describes as a chronic disease reflecting a flawed character, get better. About half of these stop drinking entirely, while the other half moderate their drinking.

Both moderation and abstinence work to address problems caused by the abuse of alcohol. What works best? That depends on the drinker, the frequency of use, and the background issues that led to the alcohol abuse or addiction.

If you drink every day, drink to wake up, or have symptoms (shakes) when you don't get a drink as usual, this book is not for you.

Some who would like to stop drinking are physically dependent on alcohol. **For those who drink every day, a detoxification program under medical supervision is the responsible thing to do.** Quitting 'cold turkey', once your body is accustomed to daily alcohol use, can be dangerous. If you're unsure, talk to your doctor about your drinking.

If your doctor thinks you're not physically addicted, you can safely try the moderation plan in the next chapter.

CHAPTER FOUR:

QUITTING: IS IT RIGHT FOR YOU:?

BEFORE YOU QUIT drinking forever, make sure that's what you want to do.

Have you tried easing up on your alcohol consumption? The 12-step model of understanding drinking problems suggests that the right solution is complete abstinence from alcohol.

Further, applying this disease paradigm to your problem drinking quickly rules out drinking less as a solution to problems with alcohol: If the problem drinker has a disease, alcoholism, the only way to recover is to avoid drinking.

This model for how we understand alcohol abuse was an improvement on the idea that it replaced, believe it or not. Before the 12-step recovery movement was launched in the 1930s, alcohol abuse was understood as a moral problem. Drunkards were pathetic, slurring staggerers who would end up as hoboes, because they lacked will power to control their drinking. In the face of that commonly 'known fact' about alcohol abuse, then, the disease model was a step forward.

However, just because you're a problem drinker doesn't mean you have a disease. You can abuse alcohol, you can even be physically and psychologically dependent on it, without having a disease that can be treated only by lifelong abstinence. Believe it or not, there are hundreds of thousands of Americans running to meetings every week, or daily, on their own or ordered there by a judge or diversion program, who have never been diagnosed as alcoholics by a doctor.

But because they haven't tried cutting back, or believe that anything less than admitting to alcoholism and entering a 12-step recovery program is 'denial', they see no alternatives.

Before you look at an online quiz and diagnose yourself with a lifelong psychological disorder, it might make sense to try moderating your drinking.

Note: If you've followed a structured moderation program and cannot effectively lessen your drinking below a threshold that causes you problems, congratulations! You're probably an alcoholic! Skip the rest of this chapter & see a doctor about safely getting off alcohol, because failing again at moderation won't make you feel healthy, powerful or capable.

Do you know how much you're drinking? Your first task is to get clear on how often, when, and with whom you're drinking. To try moderation, you have to know what you're moderating from.

1) Self-monitor For two weeks, keep a diary. Each time you drink, make a note. Where do you drink? Who is with you? How many drinks?

Make your notes as soon as you can, so that you don't lose track of what you've had. Of course, if anything interesting (fistfight, drunk dialing ex-lover, arrested for driving drunk) occurs during the time you're drinking, you'll want to make note of that too.

Keeping a diary of your drinking will help you to understand what you're doing, and identify any problems related to your use of alcohol.

2) Analyze your drinking The most serious drinking problems can be hidden in plain sight. Review your diary to look for:

- Drinking more than you intended.
- Regretting how much you drank.
- Problems with family, friends, or the law near your drinking.

If you find any of these, look deeper for any patterns. Ask yourself:

- Who was with me?
- Where was I?
- How was I feeling before I took my first drink?
- Did how I was feeling change as I drank?

If you're using alcohol to change your mood, this is a red flag.

3) Plan to moderate Knowing more about the timing and circumstances of your problem drinking, you can make better conscious choices about drinking.

Many people who use alcohol away from home find that all they need to moderate their drinking is a plan.

- How much do you plan to drink? "I plan to stop after 3 rounds tonight."
- How long do you intend to drink for? "I will go out at 9 and come home by 12."
- What can you do to help yourself follow the plan? (Take limited funds with you, etc.)
- Think of someone who will support you in your plan and enlist their support.

If your diary reflects problem drinking at home, or alone, or both, your plan will need to reflect that.

- Plan your time at home alone, with plenty of activity.
- Limit your purchases of alcohol to amounts you can drink safely (smaller bottles).

Of course, if you try moderation and find that you can't or won't lessen your drinking, to decrease problems associated with it...you may need to abstain.

CHAPTER FIVE:

UNDERSTANDING ALCOHOL: DEPRESSANT, SUGAR, HOBBY

ALCOHOL IS A depressant—except when it's a stimulant. (Yes, it's complicated.) To help you understand what happens when you drink, we'll summarize the science. Everything humans enjoy—from a good meal to sex to listening to a symphony—releases dopamine in the brain's reward pathways and trigger the release of endorphins. Alcohol affects the chemical reactions in the dopamine pathways of the brain, causing endorphins to tell the brain, 'This feels good!'

But alcohol also affects the parts of the brain controlling speech, movement and memory. It also impacts judgment, which can lead to some bad decisions under the influence. Slurred speech, unusual behavior, trouble walking and difficulty performing manual tasks can all result from excessive drinking. Long-term abuse can even shrink the frontal lobes of the brain, further impairing judgment and decision-making.

The overall impacts on neurological pathways from drinking are not yet well understood. What you need to know to manage your relationship with alcohol is simple enough: Drinking makes you feel good, at first…then it makes you feel worse. The technical term for a chemical that affects the brain this way is ' biphasic '.

As you drink, raising your blood alcohol content (BAC), alcohol acts as a stimulant. You've seen people who have one glass of wine and become 'tipsy', impulsive or silly; light drinkers, who are not in the habit of using alcohol, will feel its effects quickly.

Heavier drinkers, who use alcohol more frequently and drink more of it, often add drink after drink on top of that first pleasant buzz. As long as BAC is increasing, the brain responds to being stimulated. Once BAC begins to fall, though, the effect is a depressant one—everything seems to be slower, fuzzier and more difficult for the drinker. The old Irish proverb turns out to reflect the chemistry of the brain: 'First the man takes the drink, then the drink takes the man' is accurate enough.

Knowing that the first impact of alcohol on the drinker is a relaxing and happy one, problem drinking makes more sense. You took the first drink and felt great, right? Then the second one, while BAC was rising, felt pretty good too. It seems like as long as you keep drinking (lifting BAC), this sensation will last. But at some point, you have to stop adding alcohol. And that's when alcohol gets tricky—after two drinks or ten, BAC has to drop. You're not as happy now; you may be quite tired, but things may also seem unpleasant. Just minutes ago, you were feeling good, and now you're not so well. The depressant aspect of alcohol kicks in when BAC stops rising. Chasing that stimulant sensation, the feel-good of the first drink, is how many problem drinkers get started.

In addition to these more obvious behavioral effects, alcohol appears to change how the brain runs the body. Studies on mammals (rats, guinea pigs and even humans) show that free access to liquor seems to affect sleep/wake cycles, which are called 'circadian rhythms'. The body's clock, which is known to run in repetitive cycles from dawn to dawn in healthy people, can be reset or become dependent on alcohol to tell the user when to sleep and how often to wake during darkness. But circadian cycles don't only control sleep and waking—they also influence body temperature and hormone secretions. These settings for your body affect, in turn, how hungry you feel and dozens of other physical processes that rely on hormones being released into the bloodstream and triggering reactions throughout the body. It's possible that further studies of humans will demonstrate the 'why' of brain chemistry behind the 'what' of alcohol's apparent craftiness, working its way into the body's internal signaling.

Now that you know more about how alcohol affects your brain and body, you can think more clearly about what strategy will support you in getting sober.

CHAPTER SIX:

DRINKING AWAY YOUR PROBLEMS: IT WORKS, UNTIL IT STOPS WORKING

YOU ALREADY KNOW that your moods, coordination and sleep habits are affected by alcohol. Let's go back in time, back to your beginning with alcohol, and recall how alcohol helped you.

You may be wondering, "How could alcohol help me? My drinking is a problem. I'm reading this book because I want to change. Alcohol is bad for me, it's messing up my life, and I want to get rid of it, not understand it!"

That makes sense, except that if getting sober were a simple matter of pouring that bottle down the drain and never looking back, you'd be reading about bee-keeping or knitting or muscle cars. The reason you're here is that you have a drinking problem, and that problem didn't respond rationally to your conscious mind's sober decision to cut back or quit.

While there are dozens of scientifically tested approaches to treating problem drinking, all of them have one thing in common: They will require you to change. The best foundation for changing yourself? Understanding yourself.

If you've been told—or worse, if you tell yourself—that your continued abuse of alcohol is a sign of bad character, there is good news and bad news. The bad news is: You're not special. Many alcoholics believe that they lack will power. The good news is: You're not special, at least not in that way. Will power alone doesn't cure alcohol abuse. If you want to put an end to your problem drinking, you will need to understand exactly what your problem is.

Back to your beginning as a drinker:

When did you start using alcohol?

Drinking made you feel _____ (cool, relaxed, excited, grown-up).*

Do you have pleasant memories of time spent with friends or family, drinking?

Those are all positive things. They're happy feelings. So you began using alcohol because you tried it, you liked those feelings, and your brain remembered how good you felt.

How does your first drink make you feel now? ('Relaxed', 'normal', 'like myself' are some common answers for problem drinkers.)

Did drinking help you get through tough times?

When you are drinking, is it easier to ignore emotional issues or daily problems?

Does your drinking help you tune out your worries, or turn down your fears?

You may be surprised to learn that your brain and body have gotten used to those feelings, too. In fact, many people drink to take their minds off problems, numb out emotions or manage difficult feelings. That's normal. Alcohol may appear to be solving some problems for you, easing your moods, helping you sleep and letting you relax.

What's not normal is being unable to stop drinking, drinking at inappropriate times, and drinking that causes problems with work, family or friends. If you have those indications, your drinking is causing you problems as well as solving problems. If you're ready to quit, it's likely that the problems you're creating with alcohol are bigger than the ones you're solving.

When you began your drinking, it worked for you. Drinking was functional. Now it doesn't work. It's dysfunctional, a word you've probably heard. The particulars of your feelings—what alcohol is helping you manage, and how you can wrestle more effectively with it—is probably worth discussing with a therapist, if you see a pattern in your drinking that reflects emotional triggers for alcohol use.

Something wonderful happened recently, as part of health care reform. 'Behavioral health', or treatment for psychological or emotional challenges, is now covered by everyone's health insurance. Talk to your doctor about your desire to stop abusing alcohol, your efforts to stop drinking, and ask for a referral to a therapist. You may also find an employee assistance program at your job; that's someone in human resources whose job is to help you be productive at work by referring you to services for your health.

About therapy for alcohol abuse: In a recent textbook for therapists, 43 methods and practices for supporting sobriety were compared. The writers surveyed the available scientific studies and described what works, as measured by research, and what doesn't.

As we've already noted, 12-step programs aren't supported by sound science, but there's no reason not to try one once. They're available everywhere, practically free, and you don't need a prescription to attend.

Among therapeutic approaches, behavioral intervention and cognitive therapies seem to work well for many problem drinkers. These are short-term projects, which of course your health plan likes because they are cheaper than psychoanalysis or inpatient rehabilitation. But strangely enough, the cheap fix does work: A behavioral intervention, in the form of talking to a therapist about your drinking problem and making a plan to moderate or abstain, is useful for over half the drinkers who try it. Cognitive therapy, or behavioral training, is simply a structured form of learning about your drinking habit. Once you've tracked your drinking, as suggested earlier in this book, and looked for patterns or triggers, behavioral and cognitive therapies help you to make an action plan for how to use that information to moderate or end your drinking.

*Note that 'sleepy' and 'sick' aren't included as answers. Studies of alcoholism in families suggest that there are people whose first drink makes them tired, nauseous or anxious. Those people are at extremely low risk of alcohol abuse. Why? Simply put, they're not getting rewarded by their brains for drinking. Alcohol doesn't solve a social or emotional problem for these users—it doesn't even make them feel good. For the purposes of this self-help exercise, we're assuming that if you felt lousy when you first used alcohol, you're not reading this book—because you didn't develop a drinking problem.

CHAPTER SEVEN:

EAT REAL FOOD: SIMPLE TRICKS TO KEEP SOBER

THE FIRST AND most important tip for dietary support of your recovery: Do NOT skip meals. In fact, plan on having three to five healthy small meals a day. Many people who successfully quit drinking report that NEVER skipping a meal is one of the very best steps they took when they decided to quit drinking. There are a couple of good reasons for this suggestion.

First, drinking provided your body a regular stream of high-calorie and high-sugar simple carbohydrates. Your body got used to these "meals," and expects the pattern of calories to continue. At least at first, it is best to minimize the changes to what your body experiences as routine. In addition to keeping up the caloric rhythm that you are used to, eating 3 or 5 healthy meals a day will keep your stomach full, your blood sugar balanced, and begin to address whatever nutritional deficits your previous habit of replacing meals with alcohol may have created.

There is also another, basic reason why planning on eating so many small meals daily will help you maintain your plan to stop drinking: it will keep you busy. Whether shopping, preparing meals, sharing meals with family or friends, or planning how to improve your diet by watching the Food Channel, you will be replacing some of the time you used to spend drinking with positive plans for the healthy meals you will enjoy eating. Many ex-drinkers report that cooking is a healthy, fun, and ultimately therapeutic way to replace drinking related activities with healthy eating related activities.

Move toward maintaining a healthy diet. Often drinkers put the worst kind of crap into our bodies for nourishment. Start eating plenty of vegetables and fruit (preferably organic), lean meats, whole grains, nuts, seeds – any food that is real, unprocessed and fresh. Begin to think about ways to eat home-made, flavorful meals rather than fast food.

Junk food is quick, but will not help build the healthy nutritional foundation that your body needs. Your goal should be to eat what it takes to make you feel better, stronger, and more able to move. That diet will support your shift into a more active life, eliminate the activity and nutritional blahs, that almost certainly accompanied your drinking diet and activity level. Simply put, the healthier your diet, in general, the less you are likely to feel the need to put alcohol into your body.

It sounds too simple to be true, but there is no better alcohol avoidance miracle drug than pure, drinking water. Start drinking at least 5- 8 glasses of water each day. Your body is almost certainly somewhat chronically dehydrated and regenerating your skin, your organs, and your blood, with plenty of clean water will make a huge difference in how you feel. You can survive for weeks without food, but only a couple of days without water. One note: WATER is water. Coffee, tea, soda, juice, etc, are fine to include in your diet but they do not substitute for water. Often people who find themselves with a desire to drink, are simply unused to their body notifying them that they are in fact thirsty.

Drinking plenty of water will REDUCE your desire for alcohol. A great way to celebrate and reinforce your new powerful diet plan is to make water festive – pour it into a tall beautiful glass. Add ice, or a slice of cucumber or lemon. Make a nice pitcher of water with a few slices of fruit or berries in the bottom – all the spas do this— and then drink from the chilled pitcher throughout the day. Lemon, orange, lime, and even grapefruit or kumquat slices all work wonders to make water tasty and also have a detoxifying effect from the little but of acidic citrus in each sip.

A word about sugar: Alcohol is a sugar, so your body is used to having a lot of sugar. If you are addicted to sugar, and you almost certainly are, your body is getting it from a variety of sources, including alcohol. Sometimes, what you THINK is a temptation to drink alcohol is just your body craving sugar.

Some people find that eliminating sugar and sweets from their diet dramatically reduces their cravings for alcohol. The first three to six days of eliminating sugar can be pretty trying and tempting but many swear that the longterm reduced desire for a drink is well worth it.

Others, myself included, find that being generous with favorite sweets, even keeping hard candy in your desk drawer, or having a small (not diet) soda at hand eliminates alcohol urges. It makes sense that this works better than what is essentially giving up two addictions at once: alcohol, and the sugar that is alcohol. The sugar issue is where an unscientific survey of former drinkers I know, as well as several experts, reaches nearly zero consensus. Try what works for you. You have the power to decide that sugar helps or hinders your cravings for a drink. Personally, I have never had an embarrassing moment after grabbing a handful of M & Ms. If your reaction to the sugar-fix plan is to grab a drink on the way home, cut out the sugar, because it's not working for you.

CHAPTER EIGHT:

ENDORPHINS: GET HOOKED ON EXERCISE!

EVERYONE WILL TELL you this, and they are all correct: A moderate exercise program will make a dramatic difference in how likely you are to succeed in your plan to stop drinking.

In addition to replacing some of the endorphins you're not getting from alcohol use anymore, there are other benefits. You'll gain a lot of confidence and fresh energy from looking and feeling so much better.

Experts suggest that you set a goal of 3 or more aerobic workouts per week to begin, ideally lasting at least 20 minutes each. You know whether you should do 2 ten-minute sessions to accommodate your current state of health. The same experts seem to agree: Adding 2, but not more than 3, weight resistance workouts per week to your new fitness regime, will help your body to build new muscle, giving you new energy. So when you feel like it's a responsible move for your body…get moving!

If you're already a member of a gym, ask to see a trainer. If you haven't joined a gym, one great place to put some of that money you're saving by avoiding alcohol is a gym membership. You'll meet new people, if you attend regularly—people whose common habit is exercise! Doesn't that sound like the kind of peer group that you might gain support from hanging around?

Fitness experts focus on increasing your health, happiness, and sense of well being as you end your dependence on alcohol. They all suggest that you support your goal by de-toxifying your body, through sweaty workouts that increase the release of all the good brain chemicals that make skipping your next drink easier. They don't typically recommend types of exercise that may further your goal, unless they're selling a class or equipment for it. Consider activities that will benefit your new lifestyle choice by making new habits, new friends, or at the very least filling some of your suddenly available time.

Walking a dog is my best personal strategy. Once I leave the house with a leash I know that I can turn back, but that Pookie will enjoy our time together and I'll probably have more fun than I thought. It's at least a good deed. It also gives me less time to spend contemplating my own troubles than the treadmill or lap lane at the gym. The dog sniffs, tries to chase squirrels. Neighbors wave. It's interactive and gives me positive reinforcement (that feedback I need to support building new, better habits).

If I have a person along we can walk and talk, far away from the triggers that may have been problems for me in the past. Your mileage may vary. Perhaps you will find the contemplative time spent swimming laps to be best for your health and well being. Training for a 5k sounds miserable to me, but it may give you a whole new goal and hobby. If you are moving, your body is creating better chemistry through that movement. You can't lose.

One last critical diet and exercise suggestion. DO NOT GO ON A DIET. More people than I can count have decided that if they're going to quit drinking, and exercise, they may as well go on the long overdue diet and kill two birds with one low calorie stone. WRONG. Your body will experience a sense of starvation as you cut it off from the constant sugar and carbohydrate loading of your drinking.

The chances that you will maintain your alcohol use plan, if you are also on Cave-man Detox II, or some other low cal, or imbalanced food rationing diet, is slim indeed. Your body will quickly convert every message sent to your brain that is deprived of calories into an active craving for alcohol, a sugar that picks you up…at first.

Once you eat healthy, drink plenty of water, replace alcohol with food. Replace drinking time with some exercise and activity, you will very likely lose weight. Maybe a lot. Maybe a little. Maybe at some future point you'll decide to create a food diary, just like you did for your drinking, and discover that there are some places in your life where certain food, or eating habits are not serving your best interests.

Then, and only then, consider making reasonable, not extreme, food changes, upping your exercise regime, or both. For now, relish the fresh energy you have from eating healthier than you have, moving more than you were, and having a clear head to enjoy your renewed energy.

CHAPTER NINE:

SLEEP: THE ELEPHANT UNDER THE CARPET

ONCE YOU'VE ENDED your physical dependence on alcohol, and you're avoiding drinking, you may find that you're having a hard time getting to sleep.

The good news is: It's perfectly normal to have sleep problems after months or years of alcohol abuse. One of the common forms of damage to your body is that you may have forgotten how to sleep.

You may be wondering, How can you forget how to sleep? Well, watch a baby sometime. (If you don't have access to a baby, search online for 'videos baby falling asleep'. You'll notice right away, particularly if the baby is right there in your lap, that falling asleep by growing more relaxed until sleep begins is in fact a skill. It's a habit, you have to learn to do it, and if you've been interfering with your body's natural cycles of drowsiness and wakefulness with alcohol, you may have to start all over learning how to sleep.

The bad news is: Learning to sleep again is a steep hill to climb, for many who get sober. Whether sleep is a mountain or a mere molehill for you, you're going to have to get to the other side to stay clear of drinking.

Sleep science

For all the research that has been completed and fully understood, there is just a heck of a lot still to learn about sleep. Recent studies suggest that sleep may be your brain's wash cycle, cleaning out physical gunk; psychiatrists have long theorized that sleep, specifically dreams, give the mind a chance to organize thoughts and feelings, clearing up the waking person's awareness.

Wouldn't it be interesting if, after further study, this idea turned out to be literally true? That nighttime is the right time to freshen up both the brain (the 3 pounds inside your skull) and your mind (your awareness of who, what, where & why you are)? Right now, we just don't know what sleep is for, nor do we understand all that it does to keep you healthy. What is well-understood, though, is the importance of sleep.

Rest is vital for a healthy body and mind. Depriving enemy prisoners of sleep is considered torture…and if that baby you were watching or recalling kept you from sleeping for even a few nights, you know that's true.

So if your drinking profile includes a Yes to 'I rarely or never get through an evening without a drink', and you're experiencing sleep problems, this is a big deal. You will have major trouble staying sober without regular and deep sleep.

There are simple steps you can take to improve your sleeping abilities from 'needs improvement' to 'excellent', all on your own and starting tonight.

- When you feel tired, get into bed. If you're not sleepy, there's no benefit to lying there telling yourself that sleep is impossible for you without alcohol.
- Use your bed only for sleep (and, should you be so lucky) sex. Don't bring your phone to bed (buy an alarm clock, cheapskate!). Don't bring work to bed; review that last file in the office, not your sleep temple.
- Get out of bed at the same time every morning, weekend or weekday. Regular hours will help you get into the habit of better sleep.
- If you head to your quiet, dark, cool bedroom and aren't sleeping after 20 minutes—get up! Do something quiet, no TV, computer or other light-up screens, for 20 minutes and notice whether you're tired.
- Avoid caffeine and nicotine (coffee and cigarettes) late in the day; both are stimulants.
- If you can, avoid shift work. Changing what time you're heading to bed, and trying to sleep while it's light out, both make sleep problems worse.

But don't despair if you try all these ideas and still find yourself wishing for just one little glass of wine, or flask of Early Times, to help you sleep. That's normal, and happily, something you can get help addressing. Your sleep problem is one that medical science has devoted enormous effort to helping you manage.

Your doctor can help you to identify an appropriate medication to let you get to sleep without alcohol. For many problem drinkers, developing better sleep hygiene (habits) is a good start but not sufficient. There's never been a better time to need properly dosed, scientifically tested, medically prescribed sleep aids than now—a sleeping pill need not leave you feeling drowsy, hung-over, or dehydrated. In other words, sleep aids can work a lot better than alcohol—so if you feel that you've been misusing alcohol to help you sleep, talk to your doctor. Don't be shy about explaining the problem, and saying directly that you're recovering from alcohol abuse.

You can look forward to a bright future without drinking, in which you sleep peacefully, eat healthily and exercise regularly.

CHAPTER TEN:

GOING DEEP: DEPRESSION, ANXIETY & OTHER MENTAL HEALTH ISSUES

HERE'S A TOUGH problem: Psychological alcohol withdrawal symptoms include:
- depression
- anxiety
- irritability
- restlessness
- insomnia (difficulty sleeping)

However, many alcohol abusers have been treating these disorders with drinking! So tapering off, moderating, or ending your drinking habit can cause these emotional issues, but may also simply reveal them. If you've ended your alcohol use and depression, anxiety or insomnia continue to bother you, it's time to look at those problems on their own.

Once you decide to abstain from booze, your underlying anxiety, depression, OCD, or whatever, may become a very clear and present danger to your mental health and well being. Does being sober mean refusing all medications for common mental health problems like depression, anxiety, bipolar disorder, even schizophrenia?

Unfortunately a large number of people, especially those associated with 12-step programs, not only think so, but believe that they have a responsibility to persuade newly sober people, or even those they come across who have been sober for years, that "clean and sober" means no Wellbutrin, Prozac, no Effexor, no Klonopin, no Abilify. No matter what your underlying mental health or medical condition may be.

First, congratulate yourself. These well meaning zealots who want to play doctor—over lunch, at meetings (if you go to those), family members, and the occasional therapist—think you are doing so well at living your new empowered, healthy, sober life that they know better than you, or any medical doctor, what prescription medications you should NOT take.

Stop for a minute and consider it, though. Should drugs for mental health conditions, medical conditions that are no less biologically based, chronic, and debilitating than diabetes or heart disease be banned for you—because you are giving up alcohol? With the large numbers of studies that have demonstrated the high incidence of mental health problems among heavy drinkers and alcoholics, should you let folks talk you out of safe, effective, properly dosed treatment?

The evidence shows that well-meaning abstinence police, preaching a no-drugs, no-matter-what approach to sober living can be dangerous, to say the least. Physicians who deny needed treatment to a patient are generally vulnerable to being censured and possibly removed from practice. Do not let self-appointed sobriety police, no matter what role they play in your life, "play doctor" with your mental health. A good physician will readily help you determine whether, when, how much, and for how long, medication may be best for your mental health and safety.

When Annie had been sober for a couple of years, she felt she was facing two choices: suicide or going back to self medicating with alcohol. "When I first got sober, I was on [the antidepressant] Wellbutrin, but after a year I decided, with a bit of pressure from some of the people I knew who had been sober and were helpful in lots of ways, that I wanted to be entirely clean and sober," the 37-year-old Atlanta software sales specialist remembers.

"But when I dropped the Wellbutrin, my anxiety came back. It was worse than ever before and was becoming more severe with each passing week. I knew I was in trouble when I had trouble leaving my apartment for work —and couldn't make myself go to social functions, even church or an AA meeting. I was getting more and more paralyzed and panicked." Annie ended up seeing s sympathetic doctor who helped her determine that going back on Wellbutrin, far from threatening her stable, sober, life, was exactly what she needed to do to maintain it. "I was trying to control my brain chemistry, but that's just not possible in my case."

Three years later, Annie is newly married, and, while still sometimes situationally anxious or depressed, is hopeful and stable enough to be making plans to start a family. "I thought that the only way I could count myself as successful in being truly sober was to go without anything for my depression and anxiety. For me, that wasn't realistic or healthy."

Addiction is generally accepted to be at least partly associated with a deficiency of dopamine, a brain chemical that has a central role in the brain's pleasure and reward responses. Depression is generally believed, by current research consensus, to be caused in part by a lack of the brain chemical serotonin—the relationship is complex because the activity of the two neurotransmitters are interconnected.

According to most research-based addiction specialists, there is a mountain of evidence that links depression and alcohol abuse (other substances too, but for our purposes we'll stick to the news about your brain and booze). Depression rates are at least 3-5 times higher among people with alcohol issues than the general population. In many cases, depression, anxiety disorders, or other brain-chemistry-based mental conditions preceded alcohol use.

Self-medication, in other words was the original motivation for drinking, for many of us. A large number of people who find themselves with a drinking problem report walking a similar path. Starting from self-medication of moderate to severe depression, anxiety, or other related conditions with alcohol, they find themselves sliding away from what may have been pretty effective self-medication, to an out-of-control drinking regime with consequences that far outweigh the previous medicinal benefits the drinker experienced.

Like Annie and many other people who have stopped drinking, David tried to quit his medication, in keeping with the widespread belief in his support system: "I didn't want a crutch." he says. "My psychiatrist advised against going off my meds but it was important to me to be truly sober, so I stopped taking my pills for a year."

Abstinence from his prescribed anti-psychotic medication was not good for David's mental health. "First, I fell back into my old kind of dark depression, which is quiet obsession about things," he says. "I was still not drinking, but I couldn't seem to gain any perspective that life could be good. Nothing I tried, talking to anyone, exercising or keeping busy was helping."

David learned that for him, biology is destiny.

"I finally built up such negative, hopeless, irritated feelings and had so many thoughts that I now know were my brain chemistry out of whack, that my parents—and I'm not proud of this because I'm a 43 year-old man— told me that I could call my therapist and say, 'I think I need to go back onto medication'" or they would try to take steps to have him hospitalized.

If you are wrestling with whether your depression, anxiety or other mental health issue might benefit from anti-depressants or other physician-prescribed, and monitored medication, educate yourself about the different treatment options for your particular diagnosis and circumstance.

Your doctor, or a therapist, can help you determine whether your depression is situational, and therefore likely to moderate as you gain new skills and health away from drinking. Or whether medication for a period of time is the best way to help you reach your goals, and avoid returning to self-medication.

If your condition is chronic depression, anxiety, or other forms of mental health challenge, you need to be honest with your doctor about your concerns, and any pressures you are under to avoid medication. Stay open to the advice from a medical expert who has reviewed the scientific literature on addiction and alcoholism treatment. Wellbutrin, Prozac, other antidepressants, or specialized medications your condition indicates, may very well do more for you and your brain, to support your non-drinking life, than eking out an existence with your brain chemistry awry. Trying to avoid drinking, and simply

ignore the mental health issues that came before your drinking, works fine—
until you capitulate, self-medicate, and experience any number of bad
outcomes.

What it all comes down to, says a well-known UCLA psychiatrist, is that if
you have depression or other mental health issues independent of your alcohol
use, you will likely need to treat that depression by methods independent of just
not drinking.

Unfortunately, there are more than a few well-meaning peer supporters,
many associated with the 12-step world, who attach a huge stigma to the use of
anti-depressants as well as any and all other psychiatric medications.

Getting sober does not magically eliminate psychological symptoms, from
moderate to dangerous. "It's hard to hear people say you're not sober if you're
on antidepressants," Janice says. "I have been horribly depressed while sober,
and without my medication I wouldn't be able to work, live a normal life, and
keep myself healthy. Without the antidepressants, my depression has become
suicidal in the past, and I'm not going there again. No-one is talking me out of
the meds that have kept me alive."

David has encountered anti-medication proselytizing in many setting
where he meets and talks with other sober people. "I pretty much left each AA
group I attended, and finally quit going to meetings after the third AA group I
attended. I decided that it wasn't helping me stay sober to have the people
leading the meeting share that they didn't believe that alcoholics should use
antidepressants as a way to treat their symptoms," he says.

"To me, that's a personal medical issue, and to bring in your opinion
about it, over and over, from the podium is inappropriate. When these people
look at me, a guy who is on medications that allow my brain to function close to
normally, do they see a 'high'? I have a problem with that. I've really learned
that's a very dangerous idea, at least for me," he says.

Surprisingly, especially to some of the no-drugs-no-way clean and sober
fundamentalists , Alcoholics Anonymous has an official position of this issue—
They have a pamphlet titled "The AA Member: Medications and Other Drugs,"

the organization spells out its policy that "No AA Member Plays Doctor." As for taking medication, "it becomes clear that just as it is wrong to enable or support any alcoholic to become re-addicted to any drug, it's equally wrong to deprive any alcoholic of medication which can alleviate or control other disabling physical and/or emotional problems."

This language, put forth a bit more forcefully than in a thin, unassuming pamphlet (available only on request) might just put an end to the dangerous campaign many sobriety industry workers and 12-step volunteers and members wage against the judicious use of lifesaving mental health drugs.

This section is dedicated to John H, a great friend when he was sober and on his meds. Also to his brother Robert, who kept trying to get him help, and to the memory of his mom Geneva, his friend Ben, and the two law enforcement officers who lost their lives when the voices in John's head shouted too loudly for too long—without his schizophrenia medication to quiet them. John remained sober during the psychotic break in which he took the lives of 5 people. He is now spending what remains of his life in a state hospital for the criminally insane.

CHAPTER ELEVEN:

YOUR 7 DAY PLAN

LOSE THE BOOZE: your specific plan and strategies for successfully quitting alcohol

If you have tried to moderate your drinking unsuccessfully, or you just plain know that you are drinking heavily and are physically dependent on alcohol, it may very well NOT be safe for you to quit drinking without some assistance from a physician or other primary healthcare provider.

We are not advising medical rehabilitation, and especially not suggesting non-medical rehab facilities. **You should see a doctor and <u>level with him or her</u> about how much, how long, and what happens to you physically when you wake up in the morning, or other times that your body is short on its expected alcohol fix.**

It is mission critical that you <u>tell your healthcare provider the truth</u> about your drinking and your health. They can't help you if you tell them the same lies you've likely told yourself, your boss, or your mother-in-law. The good news about the sometimes awkward process of talking to your doctor or doctor substitute (NP, PA, CNP, etc.), about the specifics of your drinking habits and history is that the information you provide is confidential. You and your private medical information are protected under a law guaranteeing patient privacy, with a long name, The Health Insurance Portability and Privacy Act, and a short acronym, HIPPA. Period.

You may need no other medical support than a quick check-up and some encouragement. You should know, however, that there are now medications available to help treat alcoholism, whether a minor case, or the severe long-term rock bottom variety. This newer class of medicines, including naltrexone, topiramate, and acamprosate, can help you quit drinking more easily by compensating for the changes that have happened in your brain, caused by your drinking , when you quit.

These drugs, unlike the older drug (disulfiram) you may have heard of— it acted by making you incredibly sick if you took a drink— don't make you sick if you do drink. They simply outsmart your brain's pleasure and reward circuits by preventing the first drink from giving the patient that familiar feeling. These medications are not addictive and may make quitting alcohol easier by lessening the urge to drink. They can also be combined with treatment for other mental health issues like depression and anxiety, if you and your doctor pinpoint those issues as an underlying cause of your drinking.

Your primary care doctor is your first stop to treat alcohol problems, and any health issues that you have developed while drinking, Whether you decide, in consultation with the doctor, nurse practitioner, or your primary health care provider, to try a course of the new alcohol specific medications, Prozac, Wellbutrin, or other anti-depressants, or no medications at all, remember that under the new Affordable Care Act, you are entitled to have your alcohol and mental health related issues treated the same as if you arrived at the doctors office with the flu or a bad case of the mumps. If you decide to try medications, you'll probably be scheduled for several brief office visits for follow-up and support.

If you and your doctor agree that it's time to quit alcohol, and that you don't have the signs and symptoms that could lead to a serious medical event, then its' time to create and implement your lose-the-booze action plan. You can still come back to talk about any underlying mental health issues, and what medications might prove helpful, after enacting your lose the booze action plan.

Pick a date to quit.

Make sure it's within a few days, a week at most, after you've seen your doctor, and from when you sit down to create this plan. Many people find it easier to have some immediate success if their quit day is planned for a time when they will be busy with other things, like work, and isn't one of their usual major drinking days i.e. Saturday night or Friday after work's weekly beer bash. Also, and this probably goes without saying, do not plan to quit drinking on a big trigger day like the day your favorite dog died, St. Patrick's Day, New Year's Eve, the anniversary of your divorce, etc. It might seem like a great time for a new start, but it is not when you are most likely to succeed.

Make a written plan, a chart on a wall size calendar works well for some people, a journal entry with to do lists, whatever works for you. Include in your written plan the when, where, and how of your lose the booze action plan. At the very least you'll want to:

- Schedule removing the alcohol from your immediate environment, house, desk drawer, hall closet, where-ever. This house cleaning should, if at all possible happen before your target quit date as you will likely find drinking your stash easier than pouring it down the sink. If you're not the kind of drinker who has alcohol placed strategically in your environment, and already do not keep alcohol at home, at work, etc. skip this step and move on to step two.
- Tell someone you trust, besides your doctor of your plan to quit, and your planned quit date. You are looking for someone you trust who is NOT also

someone to whom you have made previous unkept promises regarding your alcohol use or other important habits. When you quit and it sticks, those closest to you will notice.

- Make a grocery list of the healthy items you will be filling your fridge and pantry with to support your body in its move toward a more healthy, post-alcohol, life. At the very least, here are some items that you'll likely find helpful to have on hand:
  - o Citrus fruits, bananas (they have lots of potassium and you are likely in need of more of this important mineral than you've been getting), berries, cherries, grapes, or other fruits that you can snack on that will even out your confused blood sugar. These also have a bit of sweetness that you will likely find helpful, as well as a good system wide cleansing effect on your poor over-worked liver and kidneys.
  - o Vegetables, pre-prepped if you are unfamiliar with your kitchen or don't trust yourself with a knife. Celery, mini carrots, cucumbers (especially the nifty miniatures that have hit the market recently), green beans, radishes, and other grabbable veggies will help add healthy items to your diet and, in the immediate term, they are additional items you can snack on to keep your mouth and stomach busy and feeling full.

    Some people report great results from grabbing some of every vegetable in the produce section, including cilantro, parsley, beets, spinach, wheat grass, etc. and running it all through a juicer 4-5 times a day, along with some citrus, for a rapid, almost certainly strong tasting, full body cleanse. Personally I would rather drink motor oil than the juice concoctions my spouse makes, but your mileage may vary and juicing may be the nutritional ticket for you.
  - o Lean meats (unless you're a vegetarian in which case you should substitute whatever nuts, seeds, tofu, cheese, etc. that you eat to add up to adequate dietary protein). Skinless chicken thighs are

lean, tasty, and very quick to prepare. A small steak may feel like a treat and it's easy and quick as well. Stir fries with meat and vegetables are a great way to return to a super healthy diet without breaking out the Julia Child cookbook.

o   Whole grain bread. Bread is bulk. It's also a carbohydrate that will help trick your body into feeling less of a loss of your former carbo-loaded alcohol diet. If you absolutely cannot stand whole grain, buy your nutrient free white bread, but make it a loaf of sourdough or French bread to add some crunch, some bulk, and some flavor.

o   Noodles, rice, potatoes, or other bulky carbohydrates. Remember, this is not the time to go on a cave-man deprivation diet. Your goal is to never feel hungry during the time you are focused on quitting drinking. A tummy with carbs feels full.

o   Nuts, seeds, wasabi peas, and other dried snacks that appeal to you. These snacks have some protein, usually a slightly salty taste, some fat, and keep your mouth busy and you feeling full. They also tend to make you want to drink more of the water you need.

o   Liquid beverages. If you follow our dietary recommendations you will be drinking 5-8 big glasses of water each day, possibly flavored with a squeeze of citrus, a few berries, or a cucumber slice. You may find that you won't need or want a whole lot of soda, juice, or other non-alcoholic beverages to add to your water regime. But buy some of what you like anyway. It's good to avoid your favorite mixers and move to root beer, orange soda, or some other juice or soda combo that you haven't associated with a strong shot of alcohol in the past.

o   Coffee, dairy, yogurt, and any snacks or meal makings with strong flavors that you like, including chips and salsa, curry, etc.

o   Sugary treats that come in small doses. If you are craving alcohol, you can often lessen or eliminate that craving with a piece of hard candy, two Oreos, spicy jelly beans, or a small dish of sherbet.

Review and respond to your sugar use early and often. Many people find that sugar is helpful to have on hand to control urges to drink; others swear off sugar because sugar makes their cravings worse or more frequent.

You'll notice that this shopping list is long on healthy items with a strong subtext of strong flavored items. When you quit drinking your mouth is likely to taste like a swamp for a while. Strong flavors, especially those from healthy acidic or spicy items will go a long way toward alleviating that awful after-taste, and make it much easier to drink all the water your body needs to clean itself out.

After you make your list, go ahead and rid your refrigerator, as much as your living situation makes practical, of artificially flavored, pre-made processed meals, diet soda, anything you usually mix with alcohol, and any other food items that you almost always have with a drink. One man's healthy whole-grain pretzel is another's nightly beer companion. Your family, assuming you live with others, will likely be quite happy to go along with your new healthier diet in exchange for all of the improvements your no-alcohol life will provide.

Drinking has very likely occupied a lot of your time. Depending on whether you've been a sociable, go-to-the-bar style drinker, a homebody watching sports on TV drinker, a secret-martyr mom drinker, or some combination of types, you will need to fill the time you have spent planning your drinking, drinking, and recovering from your drinking time.

Your quit plan, preferably on the calendar, should include scheduled exercise, probably some new, healthy activities, like cooking your healthy meals, gardening, hobbies, reading, or planning time to do enjoyable household projects or hobbies that you have neglected. You may find that it will take some time to find the activities that will both support your new alcohol-free life and be enjoyable.

Put some planned hobby time and activities on your calendar. You can always change from volunteering at the senior center to playing right field on the spring softball tam if you find that you and your interests have changed.

If, like many people, you have relied on alcohol to make social situations more comfortable or enjoyable, to manage your feelings or moods, or to deal with situations you find stressful or unpleasant, this is the time to plan healthy activities and ways to minimize your exposure to the people, circumstances, and situations that you have used alcohol to make tolerable.

~~~

Plan to avoid drinking "triggers."

There are as many different triggers as there are drinkers. But triggers, the urge to drink, generally fall into two broad categories:

External triggers are the places, events, situations, times of day, or people that remind you of drinking or offer opportunities to drink. These are high-risk triggers and are generally easy to identify, predictable, and, with some exceptions are more easily avoided than internal triggers. Wednesday night bowling, or your nightly drink with Jeopardy, lunch with your friend Ted, or the neighborhood Poker night are all examples of external triggers that you should make plans to avoid or work around.

Internal triggers can be trickier to identify, label, plan to overcome, and recognize in the moment. These internal urges to drink may just seem to come out of nowhere. But if you stop to think about when your urges to drink happen, you'll almost certainly find that some of your drinking patterns are set in motion by emotions, whether positive or negative.

Frustration, anger, stress, anxiety, fear, excitement, celebration are only a few emotions that trigger the desire for a drink in many people. You may also experience internal triggers that are caused by physical sensations such as a hunger, exhaustion, headache, tension, or nervousness. Many women report that their internal urges to drink are somewhat to heavily impacted by their monthly hormonal cycle.

Make a list of what triggers your urge to drink. <u>Do not judge your triggers, just list them.</u> Your desire-for-a-drink triggers may be certain places, people, feelings, times, or events. Be thorough, as you make an inventory of your particular triggers. They can be anything. Or any situation.

NBA play-offs may be a trigger for you. Being at the ball field, the bar, your monthly book club, or cleaning for upcoming house guests may be a trigger for you. One friend of mine gave away a set of lovely stemmed wineglasses, as they had always triggered her desire for a big round red glass of wine. Another acquaintance succeeded in staying away from her trigger event, grocery shopping, by delegating the task to her spouse for a bit and then by changing her main grocery store to a food co-op, away from the fully stocked liquor department of her neighborhood chain store.

~~~

Travel plans

If you travel for work, take special care to note your traveling triggers. Plan where you will wait at the airport, away from the bar. Make plans for where and how you will have access to healthy, frequent meals throughout your travel time. A few business people I know who travel frequently ask that the mini-bar in their rooms be cleared of alcohol before they arrive. Most hotel chains will add this to your guest profile and you'll only have to ask once. Marriott properties either do not have mini-bars or are scrupulous about adhering to guest requests to keep alcohol out of room refrigerators.

- ○ Plan a work project, take along your electronic-game toy, or take something you'll look forward to reading in your room.
- ○ Schedule exercise, it is more than likely your hotel has facilities or can provide you with access to a nearby gym or walking/running routes. Kimpton hotels, some of my favorites, have bikes available for guest use at many locations, along with yoga mats and instructional videos for use in your room. They'll even send up a goldfish to keep you company.
- ○ These ideas, and your written plans, are designed so that you spend less time alone in your room when your internal triggers to drink may be particularly strong.

If you are primarily a social situation drinker, best served in your new alcohol free life by solitary time, because you've been in the habit of frequenting after-work drinking opportunities, than by all means read quietly in your room. Rent a movie. Order a healthy meal from room service, rather than going out. Do what you need to avoid your external social triggers.

One last travel tip: whether on a business trip, your kids' school field trip, or a day at the beach: Bring snacks from your healthy and high-flavor list, or plan time to purchase these items at your destination. Most people will confront one or more of their triggers if they find themselves away from home, hungry, tired, and looking for a meal or sugar or carbohydrates.

Avoiding all triggers possible is your very best strategy. But, of course, all of us have things, places, feelings, people, etc. that cannot be fully avoided. It's pretty easy to see, with your list of triggers in front of you, what specific places, activities, times of day, or people, make you feel like having a drink. List and prepare one or more activities you can plan to do, instead of drinking, and have the planned action ready to deploy when each of the unavoidable associated triggers comes up.

~~~

Plan to handle cravings and urges to drink

When you quit drinking, it's completely normal and expected to have urges for a drink, or a craving for alcohol. Cravings and urges can refer to a virtually endless range of physical sensations, feelings, emotions, obsessive thoughts, even smells, that tempt you to have a drink, despite your committed and well planned intention to abstain from alcohol. You may momentarily forget what you plan is, or feel conflicted by the craving or urge to drink.

One of the more useful strategies we've seen for coping with sudden urges to drink is based loosely on a Cognitive Behavioral Therapy (CBT) Strategy. This is not coincidental. CBT, as it is popularly known, is the only talk therapy approach that has any significant statistical evidence suggesting that it actually increases the length and quality of sobriety in people who give up drinking and participate. No other method of therapy, 12-step, inpatient rehab groups, hypnotism or the host of other available methods has actual success rates approaching those reported by independent researchers who looked at CBT and other talk methods.

The method, commonly called by the not-even-a-bit catchy term "Recognize-Avoid-Cope", helps former drinkers, experiencing urges to drink to consciously change their own thinking patterns and reactions from ones that are clearly unhelpful to more productive thought patterns. The method can also be very helpful in uncovering internal and external triggers to drinking urges that you may not be aware of and to help you make very specific, thought and action based plans for managing them.

One piece of the CBT Recognize-Avoid-Cope strategy is to keep written track of each and every urge or craving you experience (on a worksheet made for the purpose, or even a small notebook) and then, importantly, analyze your cravings or urges to drink for a period of time, at least a couple of weeks. Once you are aware of when, where, and how you are tempted to drink, what your external and internal triggers are and how you think during periods of craving, you are well on the way to having multiple ways to avoid and lessen these attacks.

When you recognize an urge, or a craving for alcohol hits, whether or not one of your identified triggers is present, here are some immediate options:

○ At the first sign of a craving or urge to drink, whenever possible, immediately avoid the urge or whatever is triggering the craving by beginning a distracting activity. It can be physical exercise like walking around the block or ten minutes folding laundry at high speed, preparing a meal, writing a letter to your neglected Aunt Sue, or any other hobby, task, or active motion that doesn't involve drinking. You'll be most successful avoiding giving in to cravings, using the distraction method, if you come up with a range of short, mid-range, and longer options to suit the circumstances that are going on around you, and the type of trigger that you are experiencing when the urge to drink strikes.

○ Whenever possible avoid the urge by leaving any situation where an external trigger is creating your desire for a drink. You needn't vow to never attend Wednesday bowling, or go to a place where alcohol is present, but in the early days of your new alcohol free life, simply avoiding exposure to the most obvious triggers is a really good part of your lose the booze strategy.

o   Recognize the urge and cope with it. Pull a copy of your lose the booze plan out of your purse, electronic planner, or wherever you have kept a copy (oh, yes, you'll want to carry a copy initially for just this occasion).

o   Another recognition and coping strategy is to refresh your memory on the events, symptoms, or other reasons that caused you to decide to quit drinking.

o   Cope with the urge by going through any CBT, EMDR, therapy affirmations, or other tools you have found helpful until the urge passes. If you don't have enough, or effective tools, ride out the current craving and then identify some thought based tools for next time.

o   Sometimes the best way to fight off a craving to drink is to simply cope. Sit quietly, accept that the urge is only a feeling, and wait for the craving to recede. In other words, ride it like a cresting wave and experience the truth: that far from being powerless, you can experience an urge for a drink and simply wait for the wave to peak and pass.

It may not feel like it during the period immediately after you stop drinking, but the good news is that for most people cravings and urges to drink are controllable, more than a little bit predictable, and actually last very short periods of time. They also tend to rapidly decrease as your time away from alcohol builds. A bit of time and practice with your new strategies for avoiding and managing internal and external triggers should result in a lessening of the frequency and intensity of your cravings for a drink.

If your cravings do not moderate in the weeks and months after you stop drinking, you may want to revisit your healthcare provider and see if a course of one of the newer addiction control medications might be right for you. The major benefit of these meds is a reduction in uncontrollable cravings. You do not have to tough it out endlessly.

- If, after you quit drinking you find yourself depressed or anxious, know that this is entirely normal. Also know that you deserve any help you need to cope with your depression, anxiety, or other mental health issues.

- Do not take NO for an answer if you have stopped drinking and find yourself sleep deprived, moderately to severely depressed, or anxious for more than the first few days. If you are experiencing these symptoms, or any others that are causing you to have troubled or invasive thoughts, or actions, see your healthcare provider and firmly but politely request help for your symptoms.

- If your healthcare provider explains why former drinkers shouldn't take drugs for anything, under any circumstances, find a new primary care provider. You do not have to suffer through unmedicated mental or physical health problems in order to be sober.

IF AT ANY TIME YOU EXPERIENCE SUICIDAL THOUGHTS, IDEAS, OR FEEL THAT YOU ARE BEING TOLD TO HARM YOURSELF OR OTHERS, CALL 911 OR GO IMMEDIATELY TO THE EMERGENCY ROOM.

~~~

The final piece to your lose the booze, quit drinking plan: Out and about, sober.

Unless you are such a secret drinker that everyone who knows you and everyone in your community is a genuine, never before actually seen in the wild, modern-day Methodist temperance tee-totaller, sooner or later you are going to need a plan for refusing opportunities to drink.

In fact, even if you think that everyone around you is a tee-totaler, and you think (probably in error) that no one knows you drink, you still need a plan that the cliché creators, available online and at every 12-step group throughout the land, like to call "knowing your 'no'".

Nancy Reagan founded a movement on, "Just say no." Regardless of your personal politics, I think we can all agree that the simple act of saying no to alcohol or drugs is unlikely to be the end of the matter. (Or at least we can agree that if saying no to alcohol worked for you, you'd be reading some other book right now.) This is where your "no" plan comes in. Even some of the strongest personalities are surprised at how hard it can be to say, and stick to, a simple "no thank you" the first few times.

Sooner or later, very soon if you are a sociable drinker with drinking buddies, coworkers, or team-mates, someone is going to offer you a drink. You may very much want to say, "yes," or you may be feeling strong and have no hesitation in refusing. Either way, the faster you politely and briefly decline the offer, the less likely you are to waver in your commitment to not drink.

When you pause, as if considering the offer, you may open yourself up to your own internal excuses to have a drink, or you may leave yourself vulnerable to social pressure from friends or others.

You are focused on your new non-drinking life. It's important to remember that the friend, or even waitress, offering you a drink may not know you have quit drinking. The level of insistence the person offering the drink may vary as well. You may even need a series of polite to firm responses in case the person persists. Sometimes a waitress describing the latest martini in vivid detail can be just as insistent as Joe, your old bar buddy.

- "No, thank you" is a complete sentence. Anyone who keeps insisting you drink after you have said "no thank you", quickly, firmly and politely is less and less worthy of your tolerance and good cheer.

○ You do not owe anyone an explanation or excuse for declining alcohol.

○ If you choose to provide an explanation— generally I reserve this for a friend or colleague who has not seen me in a drinking situation since I stopped drinking—a simple "I'm not drinking these days, doctor's orders" is always true and appropriate.

○ Do not get drawn into a debate about whether one drink is ok for you or whether your current non-drinker status is forever.

○ If necessary walk away. Get up and leave. Change your seat. No one who continues to demand you join them in drinking, after you have politely declined, is someone you need to be next to right now.

The recognize-avoid-cope CBT strategy for handling urges and cravings described above, can also be very helpful when it comes time to resist your own, and others', pressure on you to drink.

You'll need to quickly learn to tell the difference between direct social pressure to drink— in other words, someone offering you a specific opportunity to drink — versus the indirect pressure you may feel, a craving or urge actually, to drink. These urges tend to happen when you are tempted in situations where others are drinking now or you have drunk in the past.

Initially, avoiding situations where others will expect you to drink, or you know you will be tempted to drink, may be your very best strategy. You may decide to use your urge and craving recognize-avoid-cope strategies to plan ahead for situations you cannot avoid right now. Any required work events, for instance. You may decide to arrive after the open-bar portion of the sales meeting, or re-read your reasons for not drinking in the car when you arrive at the annual awards banquet. You may even decide that you can cope with the temptation by having a good meal and a workout before the event.

Remember that any plan you make and execute, to avoid giving in to the urge to drink now, is not forever. You made a decision to quit drinking based on solid, good reasoning. You are not being punished by saying no to a drink. You may, later when your urges and cravings have fallen off, and you have more practice successfully avoiding temptation, decide that some social situations, you now wisely choose to avoid, have become safe for you and your non-drinking commitment. For now, you can use any of the strategies in your lose the booze action plan to stay distracted and busy and away from people and situations that create strong urges or social pressure to drink.

If you find, once you're stable and sober, that you miss certain friends or activities you can go two ways: Either find less alcohol-centered places and people to enjoy the old activity among, or you can stay connected with friends that you are missing, and preferably linked to by more than drinking, by calling or texting and inviting your friend(s) to join you in an activity that doesn't involve drinking. It seems to work best to suggest a new activity or meet-up location, rather than simply offering up an invite to the tee-totalers version of your old stomping grounds.

In addition to being prepared with your "no thanks," pick what makes sense to you, for the circumstances, from this list of strategies:

- Always have plenty of non-alcoholic drinks on hand at home
- Have an appropriate non-alcoholic beverage in your hand at all times, if you are in a must-attend, drinking business or social situation.
- Ask for non-alcoholic drinks, soda water, etc. to be served in a real glass, with a twist of lemon or lime. Stemware, a highball glass, or whatever everyone else at the event is drinking from, no straw please, will minimize

the number of questions you'll likely receive from others about your beverage choice, at the event.

- Insist with staff if necessary – there's nothing more conspicuous than Coke in a plastic cup at an open bar event. If they tell you that they'll have to charge you for your tonic as if it were a vodka tonic, reflect for .7 seconds on how much booze has cost you over the years, and pay up.
- Tip "as if" you'd had drinks with dinner, at restaurants where all the other tables bought a bottle a wine—you'll get excellent service, and better cooperation, next time.
- Plan an escape if the temptation gets too great.

When you successfully refuse a drink offer, note what worked, and build on it. Remember, you choose not to drink. And no one has the right to object to your choice.

You are in charge.

You know why you made the choice to quit drinking, and you know how you see your life improving with the change you have decided to make.

If you find yourself worried about what others may think, react, or see your decision to change, be aware that they are likely aware of at least some of the negative consequences of your past drinking. If they aren't aware, there is no need to fill them in or challenge their choices. Your decision is a good one for you, and should be respected. Resist any pressure to drink and seriously consider off-loading anyone in your life who sees a need to insist, draw attention to, or sabotage your plan to lose the booze.

CHAPTER TWELVE:

APPENDIX: IS REHAB FOR ME?

WHY REHAB IS worse than nothing

Did we give away the conclusion already? We wanted to touch on the 'drunk school' solution, but only after you've seen the whole picture: What alcohol does in your brain and body, what methods to stop drinking work for most people, and the specifics of how to quit for good.

Somebody is going to suggest rehab to you, at some point. Notice that this statement is not followed by any qualifiers: "if you're really messing up your life", "if you've been charged with a DUI", "if you're stinkin' drunk by 8am on weekdays". No qualifiers are needed for that statement, because rehab is big business.

As you may already know, you will not be able to search even the most innocuous terms, ideas, or suggestions for moderating your drinking—on the internet, or likely anywhere else— without someone suggesting that a stint in rehab is a necessary step to regaining control over your life.

In a few minutes we'll discuss why rehab is likely worse than doing nothing about your drinking. But first, let's take a stroll down the very-high-rent lane where the rehab companies line up to convince you, and especially your loved ones, that rehab (preferably inpatient rehab) is the right way to get sober and stay that way.

The rehabilitation and treatment services market in the United States is huge. Thanks to what is called healthcare parity (we'll come back to this in a bit), it's likely to grow at a rapid clip, too, for the foreseeable future. There is a whole sub-industry of financial and other analysts, cranking out expensive reports on just how much money is pouring through every part of the rehab world. But even industry experts don't agree within TENS OF BILLIONS of dollars how big the yearly take is. The lowest number that comes up frequently is about 8 BILLION dollars per year, with the real growth bulls claiming a current annual revenue closer to 34 BILLION dollars.

Most major rehab providers, chains like Hazelden and CRC Health Group, are privately held, meaning that they only report their earnings to their gleeful owners. Some hospital-based rehab facilities, such as those run by the Cleveland Clinic Foundation and the University of Colorado Medical Center, have given their Board of Directors an idea of how lucrative the rehab side of their ostensibly non-profit business might be— but still don't generally disclose specific numbers for "competitive" or "strategic" reasons.

State and municipal facilities are in a different budget bucket, but still create revenue for the vendors that often contract to provide the actual rehab services. About 8,000 facilities (a rough guess as no one really knows for sure whether your neighbor is providing a rehab for five adults) of various sizes, service sets, and models, are mom & pop shops that don't report their earnings to anyone but the IRS. So any number is a guess.

In addition to inpatient and outpatient rehabilitation facilities there are the myriad extra- and pseudo-rehab services such as sober living facilities, sober coaches, luxury or tough-love boarding schools for "troubled teens," week-long

"New Beginning" or "Serenity Retreats" to help you quit drinking before your boss or spouse finds out.

Many of these alternatives to Betty Ford style, "cinder block" inpatient, 12 step based rehabilitation programs, you've probably either never heard of or only read about in People Magazine. When starlet B goes into rehab for trip number 14, and comes out with a sober coach and a luxury condo at a Malibu sober living residence, it's practically a given that other facilities and entrepreneurs will soon offer these services to their slice of the market to take advantage of the publicity. Rehabilitation facilities offer ever-evolving options to spend money getting yourself or a loved one sobered up.

The rehabilitation industry has a long and illustrious, and very profitable history in this country. Sending mom or dad to "dry out" dates back to at least the 1840s, when the Temperance Movement ran Sober Houses in cities like New York and Boston. Abstinence was the goal. Residents were given a huge dose of good old fashioned religion, songs to sing, rules to follow, and generally someone of like mind to check up on them when they went back home.

At the time AA was founded in the post-prohibition 1930s, rehabilitation for alcoholics was generally offered as a religious retreat. But eventually the task of providing treatment for alcoholics was placed more and more in the hands of the medical field, leaving a lesser role for the religious and temperance societies of earlier times. Treatment moved into more clinical settings. Rehabilitation now took place in hospitals, psychiatric wards and sanitariums for treatments ranging from rest to shock treatment.

The 20th century the rise and popularity of AA created popular acceptance for the notion that treatment for alcoholics was a necessary and worthwhile endeavor that benefits society as a whole. President Richard Nixon was the first to put alcohol and other substance-abuse treatment into the federal budget during the early 1970's.

In an ironic footnote to the history of federal treatment funding, the universally well-known Betty Ford Center of Rancho Mirage, California was founded in 1982 and became the iconic rehabilitation facility for most Americans. Yet during his administration, President Gerald Ford cut President Nixon's treatment funding in half, devoting more federal dollars to the enforcement actions that would eventually be described as, "the war on drugs."

By the mid 1980s, private rehabilitation facilities were springing up across the country. Most used some form of the 12-step model popularized by Alcoholics Anonymous as the core of their treatment protocol. This is still true today, and serves a number of purposes: patients have a ready made place to go for free or low-cost follow-up care when they leave the facility. Or, the facility they've patronized can provide fee-based meetings on the step model and patient, friends and family will all know what is happening at follow-up, or "relapse prevention" meetings.

The homogenized approach of AA—with its template meeting format and rigorous policing of approved literature, meeting format, and leader behavior— means that location is no barrier to maintaining a virtually identical code of approved messaging, jargon, and routine, whether one goes to rehab in sunny Malibu or snowy Minneapolis.

With the passage of the Affordable Healthcare Act, we can expect a large number of Americans to seek referral, or to be referred by their primary care provider, to some form of medicalized plus 12-step rehabilitation services. This is true because for the first time insurance plans are required to treat mental health issues, including alcohol and other substance abuse, the same as they treat physical healthcare issues like diabetes and asthma.

Does this mean that your new Affordable Care Act approved health plan will pay $60,000 for a 28 day stay at New Start Aruba or the vaunted Cirque Lodge in beautiful no-where Utah? No.

As the new law begins to take effect, and patient rights to mental health service offerings become better known, expect to see rapid escalation of a trend, already seen as the ACA began to look like a done deal. Rehabs are moving away from the traditional 28-day, inpatient rehab program—itself a product of the length of time old-guard BlueCross/Blue Shield indemnity insurance plans would pay for inpatient stays, rather than any clinically significant magic to 28 days of sleep-away camp treatment.

The switch toward "community based" outpatient programs with lower staffing needs, virtually no licensing requirements for direct patient contact staff, and a generally, whatever the provider provides is fine with us, approach are appearing like daffodils in spring.

Without getting too far off into the technicalities of rehab services, state and federal licensing requirements, and how things have always been done, we will summarize here: Rehab is a labor intensive business. The industry prefers that the labor be inexpensive, and relies heavily on former users and abusers, as well as the huge infrastructure of the 12-step movement to minimize costs. Volunteers, like those who are leading a nearby meeting, can be relied on to meet the daily 12-step dose for rehab clients.

Some states have many more rehab programs than others. Good weather is not the only reason so many rehab facilities are located in Florida and California: these states also allow virtual self-regulation by the industry and few to no requirements for the hiring of doctors, nurses, psychiatrists, and other expensive personnel.

Expanded Medicaid rolls, along with the other ACA routes to health coverage, have rehab industry leaders meeting over-time to determine what services they will provide to absorb the new market demand of ACA plan covered patients, on a platform that will remain true to the rehab industry's underlying goal of profitability for rehab providers.

Call us cynical, but in an age when the citizens of Malibu are demonstrating and legislating at the local and state level to limit the number of luxury spa-style rehab beds in their community, it is not mere coincidence: Sudden insurance coverage, for large numbers of regular Americans with new policies but sharply limited benefits, are creating a recovery rehab boom from coast to coast. Yes, you are now entitled to coverage parity (the technical term for "an illness is an illness", whether mental or physical) but don't be surprised if your coverage gets you a visit with your primary care provider, a prescription for some anti-depressants, and a referral to your local AA meeting calendar.

The good news is that, with the exception of the referral to the utterly unproven Alcoholics Anonymous meeting program, this may not be such a bad thing. As we have discussed elsewhere, 12-step based programs have an abysmal success rate. Repackaged, branded, and marketed as expensive, "take out a second mortgage if you really love her" inpatient rehab programs, do not make 12 step or other programs based on little or no research any more effective. Studies have even been done to determine whether spending big bucks on rehab encourages longer periods of sobriety in the luxe program graduates. Short answer: No.

All that going to an elite rehab will guarantee, with 100% certainty, is that you will receive constant, beautifully-produced glossy mail, and online communications, from the rehab facility you bought from, graciously inviting you to come back for another sobriety-seeking vacation, at retail, of course, whenever you are once again in need.

Yes, they're that confident in the effectiveness of their programs, and you'll also be solicited by the competitors you didn't use, who are equally aware that the product they sell isn't effective. These marketing pitches may also gently suggest, repeatedly, that you observe other family members for tell tale signs that they might benefit from a five-figure stay at dry-out camp.

Please note here that we are not suggesting that there are no tools, medical interventions, therapeutic modalities, etc. to help you keep your vow to get and stay sober. We are simply saying that the research states two things unequivocally:

1)   Inpatient residential, or highly supervised outpatient rehab, regardless of whether it is in the currently in vogue spa style packaging, with a gourmet chef and Pilates, or the old-guard everyone-cleans-toilets, Betty Ford, "cinder block" model, has absolutely no statistically proven impact on whether you will remain sober once leaving the care of the facility.

As someone once said, there are lies, damn lies and statistics. Follow-up care, relapse prevention, and success rate statistics provided by every rehabilitation program in business, for profit or not, are utterly unconvincing. In fact, double-blind, unbiased academic research showing the complete lack of evidence that the programs or their promised extras will be effective in your quest for a sustained and sustainable sober life.

2)   Luxury, cinder-block, and prison rehabilitation programs are, in every important detail, identical. 84% of rehabs surveyed in 2012 indicated that they adhere closely to a 12-step treatment model, with a bit of their own branded special lingo thrown on top. Fewer than 20% of facilities offer any medications or other specialized treatment for the kinds of mental health problems that likely underlie your drinking.

If you like the views in Malibu and can afford the freight, great. But when you leave you will need to employ the same tools and techniques to stay sober as someone who stayed home and kept the money in the bank. If you have already tried rehab, or even local 12 step meetings and have not been successful, do not expect a fresh stay a Club Sober to change your outcomes.

Chapter Thirteen:

Resource Guide

Most people who want to get sober stop drinking on their own. Despite the claims of Alcoholics Anonymous and the host of rehab facilities advertising their services, you may very well succeed at losing the booze simply by following the suggestions in this book, and trusting yourself to follow through on your moderation or abstinence commitment, because you know it's best for you.

That said, since 'Lose The Booze' first came out on Kindle, we have received many inquiries via email and on the Lose The Booze blog, asking for recommendations for recovery and rehabilitation services that aren't 12 step based.

There is absolutely nothing wrong with deciding that your moderation or sobriety journey will go better for you with some assistance from a private therapist, specializing in research based cognitive behavioral therapy (CBT), EMDR, or other approaches that put you in the drivers seat and encourage your positive choices.

You may also be someone who has the need, and has the resources, to take time away from your day-to-day life to focus on you and your sobriety. Finding inpatient rehabilitation facilities that offer non 12-step programming can feel like looking for a needle in a Betty Ford haystack.

So in this revised, second edition of Lose the Booze, we've hunted down a selection of non-step rehab facilities. There are a dizzying array of options out there! They range from semi-traditional luxury rehabilitation facilities with CBT and medical oversight instead of 12 step meetings, to Zen and other spiritual retreats that offer self-reflection, great cuisine, and varied approaches to achieving long-term health. Demand for non-12 step-rehab and moderation and abstinence support services is exploding, and new offerings are popping up constantly.

When calling any facility you should confirm that you are seeking a non-12 step program. Many of the larger rehab chains offer step programs and non-12 step programs, sometimes even in the same facility. More often the non-step offering is in a separate unit or facility but you'll want to confirm and verify service specifics, to make certain that you're not being slotted into a 12-step-light version of the same old step rehab option.

A note about rehabs and advertising: in the process of identifying non-12 step rehab and therapy facilities, both inpatient, and outpatient, we found dozens of online sources for rehabilitation referral services. We also found voluminous directories of rehabs with pictures, menus, and patient reviews.

Please keep in mind that the online guides are advertiser supported, and/or receive a fee from the rehabilitation facility for every potential patient referral that is generated through the 800 number or online referral form. We're not against advertising or referral fees in principle, but when you are searching for a rehabilitation facility you deserve to receive unbiased, un-varnished, information about the program, the facility, the staff, etc.

The Lose The Booze Rehabilitation and therapy directory is purposely bare-bones. We receive no payment of any kind from the listed professionals or facilities. This leaves it to you to evaluate each program we list, using their direct contact information instead of a paid review.

If you find other non-12 step facilities, or discover that entries on this list have shifted away from the non-step focus they offered in May 2014, please let us know so that we can update future editions.

Each entry in the directory is arranged in the following order:
Name of Treatment Provider/Program
Program Administrator & Title
Provider Type
State
City/Province
Country
Web Site
Phone

Alcohol & Drug Addiction Treatment
Jason Thomas, COO
inpatient
California
Calabasas
United States
http://www.prominencetreatment.com
(866) 220-0863

Allied Counseling Group
Kristin L. Milne-Glasser, LCADC, Clinical Director
outpatient
Maryland
Fredrick
United States
http://www.alliedcounselinggroup.com
(301) 698-7077

Alternatives Addiction Treatment
Marc F. Kern Ph.D.
Outpatient Treatment Facility
California
Beverly Hills
United States
http://www.AddictionAlternatives.com

(888) 532-9137

Anderson (Andy) Orr, M.Ed., MRE, LCAS, LAT
Anderson (Andy) Orr, M.Ed., MRE, LCAS, LAT
solo provider
North Carolina
Raleigh
United States
http://www.reasonforrecovery.com
919-274-8001

A Positive Alternative
Catherine Trestrail, CDP, MSW, ACSW
outpatient
Washington
Seattle
United States
http://www.apositivealternative.com/
206-547-1955

ARCA Midwest
Percy Menzies
Inpatient/Outpatient Treatment
Missouri
St. Louis
United States
http://www.arcamidwest.com/
314-645-6840

ARCA Georgia
Terry Bruce
Inpatient/Outpatient Treatment
Georgia
Savannah
United States
http://www.arcageorgia.com/
(888) 570-6391

Assisted Recovery Center
Fred Rector
Outpatient Treatment
Arizona
Phoenix
United States
http://www.assistedrecovery.com/
(800) 527-5344

ATI Wellness - eEnliven
Charles C. Robinson, MA, LMHC
Inpatient Treatment Facility
Clearwater
Florida
United States
http://www.alternative2rehab.com/
727-223-8911

AToN Center
Leslie Sanders, Psy,D, PSY25665 Program Director
Inpatient Treatment Facility
California
Encinitas
United States
http://www.atoncenter.com
(888) 535-1516

Avalon Malibu
Jeff Schwartz, LCSW
Inpatient Treatment Facility
California
Malibu
United States
http://www.avalonmalibu.com/
(888) 958-7511

Balance Treatment Center
Ronald Sager, M.D.
Treatment Facility
California
Calabasas
United States
http://www.balancetreatmentcenter.com
1-855-414-8100

Casa Palmera
Anissa Bell
Outpatient Treatment Facility
California
Del Mar
United States
http://casapalmera.com
866-768-6719

Blu By the Sea
Randy and Debbie Ross
Inpatient Treatment Facility
Florida
East Destin
United States
http://www.blubythesea.com/
1 (877) 589-3268

Brian Whitley, M.A., LMFT
Brian Whitley, M.A., LMFT
solo provider
California
Irvine
United States
http://www.BrianWhitley.com
949-933-5872

Calabasas Recovery
Beth Geyer CPC
Solo/outpatient
California
Calabasas
United States
http://www.calabasasrecovery.com
Via website form

Center for Family & Adolescent Research
Erica Finstad, PhD
Treatment Facility
Oregon
Portland
United States
http://www.ori.org/CFAR/Portland/
(503) 243-1065

Chapters Capistrano
Michael Shea
Treatment Facility
California
San Clemente
United States
http://www.chapterscapistrano.com
949-307-3879

Cognitive and Behavioral Therapies

Dr. Robert Heller
solo provider
Florida
Boca Raton
United States
http://www.cognitivetherapy.cc
561.451.2731

Cornerstone Recovery Center
Robert J. Scardino, CAP
Outpatient Treatment
Florida
Ft. Lauderdale
United States
http://www.cornerstonefl.com
888-711-0354

Creating Healthy Alternatives Together
Cliff Koblin, MA, LPC, LCADC
Solo
New Jersey
Kingston
United States
http://www.cliffkoblin.com
(609) 333-1096

Creating Healthy Alternatives Together
Cliff Koblin MA, LPC, LCADC
Solo
New Jersey
Branchburg
United States
http://www.cliffkoblin.com
(609) 333-1096

Daniel Khan Coaching
Daniel Khan
Solo Provider
Richmond Hill
Ontario
Canada
http://www.sarecovery.com

David Gibbs M.A., LMHC, CAP
David Gibbs M.A

Solo/Outpatient
Florida
Port St. Lucie
United States
None
(772) 672-3193

Desert Canyon Recovery Center
None listed
Inpatient Treatment Facility
Arizona
Sedona
United States
www.desert-canyon.com
(888) 811-8371

Enterhealth Ranch
David M. Kniffen, Jr
Inpatient
Texas
Van Alstyne
United States
www.enterhealth.com
(800) 388-4601

Enterhealth Outpatient Center of Excellence
David M. Kniffen, Jr
Outpatient Treatment
Texas
Dallas
United States
www.enterhealth.com
(800) 388-4601

JACQUELYN SMALL, LMSW"
28 day recovery center
Texas
Austin
United States
http://www.eupsychia.com/
(512) 327-2795

Gary Vann, PhD
Gary Vann, PhD, Director
solo provider
Michigan

Traverse City
United States
http://www.garyvannphd.com
231-947-2990

Grace Counseling Center
Cheryl Rayl, MS, LPC, MAC
Outpatient Treatment Facility
Texas
Lewisville
United States
http://grace-counseling.com/
(800) 972-0643

The Healthy Lifestyles Guided Self-Change Program
Dr. Linda Sobell & Dr. Mark Sobell, Co-Directors
outpatient
Florida
Ft. Lauderdale
United States
http://www.nova.edu/gsc
(954)-262-5968

Harbor House, Inc.
Jimmie A. Wooding, LCSW
Treatment Facility
Arkansas
Fort Smith
United States
http://www.recoveryhhi.org
479.785.4083

Henry Steinberger, Ph.D. LLC
Henry Steinberger, Ph.D.
Outpatient
Wisconsin
Madison
United States
http://smart-recovery-intro.blogspot.com/
608) 247-5199

Inspire Malibu
Dr. Akikur Mohammad, MD
Treatment Facility
California
Agoura Hills

United States
http://www.inspiremalibu.com
(866) 220-0863

J. Richard Crossfield, LMHC, MAC
Rich Crossfield, Psychotherapist
Solo practitioner
Florida
Jacksonville Beach
United States
http://www.jrcrossfield.com
(904) 853-5900

Jamie Downs, MSW, LGSW, ADC/ Holistic Therapy Center
Jamie Downs, MSW, LGSW, ADC/ Director/Certified SMART Recovery
Facilitator
solo
West Virginia
Morgantown
United States
http://www.holistictherapyctr.com
304-680-7003

Jean M. Alberti, Ph.D.
Jean Alberti, Ph.D., Clinical Psychologist/Owner
solo provider
Illinois
Glen Ellyn
United States
http://therapists.psychologytoday.com/13208
(630) 354-8868

Jessi Frothingham, LMFT, Certified CRAFT Therapist
Solo, Outpatient
Oregon
Portland
United States
http://www.jessifrothingham.com
971-295-3654

Jonathan von Breton, LCMHC
solo provider
Rhode Island
Smithfield
United States
(401) 349-4997

Journey Malibu
Arielle Penn
Treatment Facility
California
Malibu
United States
http://www.journeymalibu.com
877-890-3627

Katie Brooks, LCSW
Solo
California
Solana Beach
United States
http://www.Goodtherapysandiego.com
(760) 525-9565

Kaufman Counseling Center
Lawrence B. Kaufman LMFT, CAP, SAP
solo provider
Florida
Boca Raton
United States
http://www.kaufmancounseling.com/
561-302-0568

Kolmac Clinic (An intensive outpatient treatment facility)
George Kolodner, MD
Outpatient
Maryland
Silver Spring
United States
http://www.kolmac.com
(301) 589-0255

Kolmac Clinic (An intensive outpatient treatment Facility)
George Kolodner, MD
outpatient
Maryland
Columbia
United States
http://www.kolmac.com
(301) 589-0255

Kolmac Clinic (An intensive outpatient treatment facility)
George Kolodner, MD
Outpatient
Maryland
Towson
United States
http://www.kolmac.com
(301) 589-0255

Maija Ryan, LCSW
Solo Provider/Outpatient
Oregon
Portland
United States
https://sites.google.com/site/maijaryantherapist/
503-444-8227

Malibu Horizon
Dr. Akikur Mohammad M.D.
Inpatient
California
Malibu
United States
http://malibuhorizon.com
(818) 889-4444

Michael Ascher M.D.
Solo Provider/Outpatient
Pennsylvania
Bala Cynwyd
United States
http://www.AscherMD.com
646-812-1421

Muscala Chemical Health Clinic
Robert M. Muscala, R.N.
Outpatient Treatment Facility
Minnesota
Edina
United States
http://www.muscala.com/
(952) 920-1351

Nancy Handmaker, Ph.D.
New Mexico
Corrales

United States
(505) 336-0432

New Roads Treatment Centers
Peter Busch - Director of Communications
Treatment facility
Utah
Orem
United States
http://www.newroadstreatment.com
888-357-3101

Non 12step Rehab
Robert Mauer
Website Information Service
Arizona
Tucson
United States
http://www.non12step-rehab.com
Web site form

Olympia House
Dr. Wayne Thurston PSY 17829
Inpatient Treatment Facility
California
Petaluma
United States
http://www.OlympiaHouseRehab.com
888.795.1965

Outpatient Substance Abuse Programs
Ryan Paul Carruthers, Executive Director
Outpatient
Nebraska
Omaha
United States
http://www.abintracenter.com
402-933-1504

Pavillon Foster Addiction Rehabilitation Centre
Jennifer Mascitto, Director of Professional & Rehabilitation
Inpatient/Outpatient Treatment
Montreal, Quebec
Canada
http://www.pavillonfoster.org
514 486-1304

Practical Recovery
A. Thomas Horvath, Ph.D.,
Multiple Services
California
La Jolla
United States
http://www.practicalrecovery.com/smart-recovery/
800.977.6110

Professional Recovery Counseling, LLC
Jo Abney, NCC, LPC
Outpatient
Georgia
Cumming
United States
http://www.professionalrecoverycounseling.vpweb.com
770-630-6892

Prominence Treatment Center
John Navab
California
Beverly Hills
United States
http://www.prominencetreatment.com/
(877) 383-2284

Ralph D. Raphael, Ph.D.
Ralph D. Raphael, PhD
solo provider
Maryland
Baltimore
United States
http://www.ralphraphael.com
410.825.0042

Rational Treatment Services
Richard Sirota, CDP, LICSW, Clinical Supervisor
Outpatient Treatment Facility
Washington
Seattle
United States
http://www.RationalTreatmentServices.com
206-459-2242

Rational Treatment Services

Richard Sirota, CDP, LICSW, Clinical Supervisor
Outpatient Treatment Facility
Washington
Bellevue
United States
http://www.rationaltreatmentservices.com
206-459-2242

Resolutions Unlimited
Michael S. Shear, Psy.D.
solo provider
Illinois
Peoria
United States
http://resolutionsunlimitedinc.com/
(309) 673-9385

Robert J. Kennerley, PhD
Robert J. Kennerley, PhD. PA
solo provider
Florida
New Smyrna Beach
United States
http://www.ccnsb.com/
(386) 423-9161

Rutgers-The State University of NJ
Noelle Jensen, MSW-Project Coordinator
Center of Alcohol Studies
New Jersey
Piscataway
United States
http://alcoholstudies.rutgers.edu/
(848) 445-2190

Saint Jude Retreats
Mark W. Scheeren, Chairman & Co-Founder
Inpatient Treatment Facility
New York
Amsterdam
United States
http://www.soberforever.net/
1888.424.2626

Schick Shadel
Bruce Brandler

10-day inpatient
Washington
Seattle
United States
schickshadel.com
1 (888) 980-6206

Serenity Malibu
Dr. Sheila Shilati
Inpatient Treatment Facility
California
Malibu
United States
www.serenitymaliburehab.com/
888.886.6475

Serenity Treatment Center, Inc.
Christine R. Marquardt
Outpatient Treatment
Maryland
Frederick
United States
http://www.serenitytreatmentcenter.com
301.898.2627

Sibcy House
Kathleen Neher-Admission Coordinator
Inpatient Treatment Facility
Ohio
Mason
United States
http://www.sibcyhouse.org
(513) 536-0537

Sobriety Home Foundation
Catherine Cosgrove
Inpatient Treatment Facility
Godmanchester
 Quebec
Canada
http://www.sobriety.ca
1-877-777-4386

Sovereign Health of CA
Dr. Lesley Davis, PsyD., MFT
Treatment Facility

California
San Clemente
United States
http://www.sovereignhealthgroup.com
(949) 369-1300

St. Gregory Recovery Program
Clayton Walters, Vice President of Operations
Inpatient Treatment Facility
Iowa
Des Moines
United States
http://www.StGregoryCtr.com
866.782.0290

Steven B. Singer, M.Ed., LPC
Provider
Virginia
Winchester
United States
http://www.sbsingerlpc.com
(540) 662-2202

Summit Estate
Jerry Callaway, M.D.
Inpatient Treatment Facility
California
Los Gatos
United States
http://www.summitestate.com/
(800) 701-6997

Suncoast Rehabilitation Center
Tammy Strickling
Inpatient Treatment Facility
Florida
Spring Hill
United States
http://www.suncoastrehabcenter.com
888-802-7218

The Kolmac Clinic (An intensive outpatient treatment facility)
George Kolodner, MD
outpatient
District of Columbia
Washington

United States
http://www.kolmac.com
(301) 589-0255

The Path of Greatest Advantage
William Dubin, Ph.D.
Solo Provider/Outpatient
Texas
Austin
United States
http://www.souldirected.com
(512) 343-8307

The Sanctuary at Sedona
Dean Taraborelli
Inpatient Treatment Facility
Arizona
Sedona
United States
http://sanctuary.net/
928-639-1300

The Thought Exchange
Rich Dowling, M.A., LPC, MAC
Outpatient
New Jersey
Morristown
United States
http://www.thethoughtexchange.biz
(973) 984-8244

The Zen Recovery Path
Sifu Matthew
Inpatient/Outpatient Treatment
California
Costa Mesa
United States
http://www.zenrecoverypath.com/

Turning Point Centers
Joe Kealamakia
Inpatient/Outpatient Treatment
Utah
Sandy
United States

http://turningpointcenters.com/non-12-step-based-rehab/
(801) 576-0745

Holistic Light
Vladimir Kogan
Inpatient Treatment Facility
Samara Beach
Costa Rica
http://www.holisticlight.com
(888) 236-3296

Holistic Light
Vladimir Kogan
Inpatient Treatment Facility
Boquette
Panama
http://www.holisticlight.com
(888) 236-3296

Will Froilan, Ph.D., LSW
Dustin Mets, CEO-CompDrug, Inc.
Outpatient Treatment Facility
Ohio
Columbus
United States
http://www.compdrug.org
(614) 224-4506

Your Empowering Solutions, Inc.
Mary Ellen Barnes, PhD., Edward W. Wilson, PhD., Program Director
Outpatient Treatment Facility
California
Rolling Hills Estates
United States
http://www.non12step.com
888-541-6350

Sierra Tucson
Stephen Fahey, M.S.W., M.B.A.
Inpatient Treatment Facility
Arizona
Tucson
United States
http://sierratucson.crchealth.com/
(866) 897-3137

Scottsdale Recovery
Chris Cohn
Inpatient Treatment Facility
Arizona
Scottsdale
United States
http://scottsdalerecovery.com/
(888) 309-3385

Sundance
Dr. Ravi Chandiramani
Inpatient Treatment Facility
Arizona
Scottsdale
United States
http://www.sundancecenter.com
(866) 677-7213

Printed in Great Britain
by Amazon